D0471486

Flashpoints!

Plays About Controlling Anger

By Catherine Gourley

CRABTREE
Publishing Company
www.crabtreebooks.com

Crabtree Publishing Company

www.crabtreebooks.com

Project coordinator: Kathy Middleton
Editor: Reagan Miller
Proofreader: Molly Aloian
Production coordinator: Ken Wright
Prepress technician: Amy Salter

Written, developed, and produced by
RJF Publishing & A+ Media

Project management: Julio Abreu,
  Robert Famighetti
Managing editor: Mark Sachner
Associate editor: Anton Galang
Design: Westgraphix LLC/Tammy West
Illustrations: Spectrum Creative, Inc.

Library and Archives Canada Cataloguing in Publication

Gourley, Catherine, 1950-
    Flashpoints! : plays about controlling anger /
Catherine Gourley.

(Get into character)
ISBN 978-0-7787-7362-7 (bound).--ISBN 978-0-7787-7376-4 (pbk.)

    1. Anger--Juvenile drama. 2. Children's plays,
American. I. Title. II. Series: Get into character

PS3557.O86F53 2010   j812'.54   C2009-906778-1

Library of Congress Cataloging-in-Publication Data

Gourley, Catherine, 1950-
 Flashpoints! : plays about controlling anger / by Catherine
Gourley.
    p. cm. -- (Get into character)
 ISBN 978-0-7787-7376-4 (pbk. : alk. paper) -- ISBN
978-0-7787-7362-7 (reinforced library binding : alk. paper)
 1. Anger--Juvenile drama. 2. Children's plays, American.
I. Title. II. Series.

PS3557.O915F53 2009
812'.6--dc22

                                        2009047081

Crabtree Publishing Company

Printed in the USA/122009/BG20091103

www.crabtreebooks.com   1-800-387-7650

**Published in
Canada
Crabtree Publishing**
616 Welland Ave.
St. Catharines, ON
L2M 5V6

**Published in the
United States
Crabtree Publishing**
PMB 59051
350 Fifth Avenue, 59th Floor
New York, New York 10118

**Published in the
United Kingdom
Crabtree Publishing**
Maritime House
Basin Road North, Hove
BN41 1WR

**Published in
Australia
Crabtree Publishing**
386 Mt. Alexander Rd.
Ascot Vale (Melbourne)
VIC 3032

Series Consultants

Reading Consultant: Susan Nations, M.Ed.; Author/Literacy Coach/Consultant in Literacy Development, Sarasota, Florida.

Content Consultant: Vinita Bhojwani-Patel, Ph.D.; Certified School/Educational Psychologist, Northfield, Illinois.

Contents

Note to the reader: Be sure to look at the Glossary on page 32 to find definitions of words that might be unfamiliar.

Striker

Corey Ramos dreams of being an all-star striker and going on to play soccer in high school. His explosive temper might just trip him up, however. When he doesn't score on the playing field, he takes it out on others. Will Corey's short fuse burn out his dream?

Characters:

Narrators 1, 2, 3

Corey Ramos, *a seventh-grade soccer player*

Becca Ramos, *Corey's nine-year-old sister*

Kelly Jordan, *sports trainer*

Paul Iorio, *Corey's rival for striker*

Coach Wells

Alex, *soccer player*

Parent

Scene 1

Narrator 1: In the final two minutes of the soccer match, Waterville Middle School leads West Side Middle School, 4 to 2. West Side's ace striker Corey Ramos is in position, close to the Waterville goal.

Narrator 2: Corey fakes a kick, but the defender isn't fooled. Corey loses his balance, twists, and falls hard. Quickly, he's back on his feet. But a stabbing pain in his right ankle topples him again.

Narrator 3: On the sidelines, the trainer examines Corey's ankle.

Kelly: Looks like a lateral ligament.

Corey: What does that mean?

Kelly: You've got an ankle sprain.

Corey: It doesn't hurt. I can still play. Can you tape it?

Coach: No way, Corey. This game's over for you. Where's the new kid? Iorio! You're in.

Narrator 1: Corey slams his fist on the bench.

Kelly: Easy! You want to fracture your wrist, too?

Narrator 2: Paul Iorio is also a striker, but with Corey on the team, he hasn't gotten much field time. Now, in the final minutes of the match, he attacks the goal and scores.

Alex: GOAL! Whoa! Corey, did you see that move? Iorio's good!

Corey: *(speaking under his breath)* That should be me out there! Not some sixth grader.

Narrator 3: Time is against West Side today, however. The clock runs out, and they lose the match by one point. Corey throws his water bottle to the ground in anger and hobbles off the field with the help of the trainer.

Corey: Talk about a stupid move. My kid sister plays better than I did today.

Kelly: Don't beat yourself up. There were ten other guys on the field with you. You didn't lose the game.

Narrator 1: Knowing that doesn't make Corey feel any better, just more angry with himself.

5

Scene 2

Narrator 2: On Monday, Corey comes to practice on crutches. He sits on the bench and watches the action. He has opinions on everything and shouts at his teammates.

Corey: Quit chasing the ball, Alex! You're running around like a lost dog.

Alex: Hey, Ramos. Back off!

Coach: *(to Kelly)* Iorio has the height to be good at headers, but he's not very muscular. If we play him, the opposing defenders are going to hit him hard.

Kelly: He's tougher than he looks. He can handle it.

Narrator 3: Corey hadn't paid much attention to Paul during practice. Now that Corey is benched with an injury, he can see that Paul is good. And fast!

Corey: *(angrily)* I've got to get back in the game!

Narrator 1: But on Saturday, he is on crutches—and on the bench.

Coach: *(to Paul)* These players are older and bigger than you. Just control the ball. Don't try to out-muscle anyone.

Narrator 2: Once on the field, Paul doesn't hold back. He is lightning fast and scores two goals in the first half.

Narrator 3: Corey watches as his teammates jump on Paul, congratulating him. Something inside Corey tightens.

Corey: *(mutters to himself)* But I'm the star striker. I've always been the best.

Alex: *(teasing)* That ankle better heal quick, Ramos, or you'll be on the bench for good!

Corey: *(angrily)* That'll never happen!

Scene 3

Narrator 1: A week later, Becca is in the backyard practicing her footwork. Corey watches. He no longer has crutches, but his sore ankle keeps him from playing with her.

Corey: You've got to train your feet, Becca! Don't you get it?

Becca: I'm trying! It's not easy. I'm not as good as you are. *(pauses)* Hey, you coming to my game tomorrow?

Corey: Wouldn't miss it. You're my star pupil.

Narrator 2: Becca fakes passing him the ball. Instinctively he goes for it, but the pain in his ankle makes him wince. Frustrated, he knocks over the goal and limps away.

Becca: *(calling after him)* Where are you going? Corey, you said you'd help me get ready for my game!

Narrator 3: Corey enters the house, slamming the door behind him.

Scene 4

Narrator 1: Monday after school, Corey stands—without his crutches—on the sidelines at Becca's game.

Corey: *(shouting)* Open your eyes, Becca! You're missing passes. Hustle, come on!

Parent: Cool down, buddy. They're just kids. It's supposed to be fun.

Narrator 2: At the half, Corey tells Becca what she's doing wrong.

Corey: Don't just stand there and wait for the ball, Becca. You have to be aggressive. Attack it, head it with power. Don't be afraid of the defenders.

Becca: *(sounding hurt)* I'm not afraid.

Corey: Then what's your problem?

Narrator 3: Becca hangs her head. Her brother's criticism is hard to take.

Becca: I'm not as good as you, Corey. I can't play like you.

Corey: Sure you can. You're just not trying hard enough!

Paul: Hey, Ramos! Hi, Becca. Good game, huh?

Corey: Good game? If your kid sister was playing on the winning team, maybe.

Paul: *(laughing)* My kid sister *is*!

Narrator 1: Corey feels that same tightening in his stomach, like he wants to lash out and break something. Is Paul *trying* to make him feel bad?

Paul: So, how's the ankle?

Corey: What do you care?

Paul: You don't have your crutches, so I just thought—

Corey: You may be the ace striker now, Iorio. But it'll be over on Saturday, because I'm going to play.

Narrator 2: The game whistle sounds. The second half is about to begin.

Paul: I guess we'll see on Saturday. I'm just happy to get in some playing time. Sorry you had to get hurt for that to happen.

Narrator 3: Corey just glares at Paul.

Paul: *(shrugs)* Okay. . . . Catch you later, I guess.

Narrator 1: Once Paul is gone, Corey suddenly feels guilty for the way he spoke to Becca.

Corey: I'm sorry, Becca. I didn't mean to shout at you.

Becca: I'm used to it. Just . . . you know, don't embarrass me in front of my friends, okay?

Corey: *(confused)* Embarrass you? How do I embarrass you?

Narrator 2: Becca rejoins the team without answering.

Scene 5

Narrator 3: On Saturday, West Side Middle School plays St. Patrick's Middle School. The winning team will advance to the district play-offs.

Narrator 1: Corey is suited up. The trainer examines his ankle.

Kelly: That hurt?

Corey: No.

Kelly: Would you tell me if it did?

Corey: *(grins)* No.

Kelly: You can play, but not hard, and not long.

Narrator 2: Coach is cautious with Corey. He pulls him out to rest him. Paul is now on the field. West Side is winning. Paul is making some exciting moves. And then . . .

Narrator 3: A player fouls Paul, but the referee doesn't hold up the yellow warning card.

Corey: *(to Coach)* Did you see that? Why didn't he call it?

Coach: Cool down, Corey. It's okay.

Narrator 1: But Corey doesn't cool down. He carries his anger onto the field when Coach puts him in again. Corey aggressively attacks the ball, but the defenders are all over him.

Narrator 2: Frustrated, he pulls an opponent's shirt. The referee holds up a yellow card.

Corey: Aw, come on! *(to referee)* How come you can see that, but you can't see it when one of our guys gets fouled?

Alex: Back off, Corey! He'll kick you out of the game.

Corey: Don't tell me what to do!

Narrator 3: Play resumes. Within seconds, Corey and an opposing player make contact. Corey pushes himself free of the other player, who falls to the ground and grabs his knee. The referee holds up a second yellow card and points it straight at Corey.

Narrator 1: With two fouls, Corey is out of the game for good.

Narrator 2: Corey loses all control. He points at the opposing player, screaming:

Corey: Faking! He's faking!

Narrator 3: Alex tries to hold Corey back, but Corey shoves him to the ground.

Scene 6

Narrator 1: West Side has lost the game. The season is over. There will be no play-offs.

Narrator 2: Inside the locker room, the players are upset. No one speaks to Corey.

Corey: I'm *sorry*, okay? I just lost it. But the ref was wrong!

Alex: No, Corey. You were wrong! And you know what else? You made us all look bad!

Narrator 3: Corey wonders, Is this what Becca meant when she said he embarrasses her? He makes her look bad?

Corey: I wasn't thinking. I just reacted.

Coach: Okay, guys. We'll talk on Monday. I want to speak to Corey here, alone.

Narrator 1: The boys gather their gear and leave. Corey sits on the bench, bracing himself for a lecture on sportsmanship.

Corey: The ref was wrong, Coach. The other guy was faking!

Coach: Maybe he was, and maybe he wasn't. That's not why we lost the game. You lost the game for us. Your anger lost the game for us.

Corey: I know, I know. If I hadn't fouled, then the other team wouldn't have gotten those penalty kicks and scored.

Coach: (softly) You're wasting your talent, Corey. Soccer is more than speed and strength and hard work. Soccer's a brain game. You know what that means?

Corey: (sighs) Yes. Tactics. All those Xs and arrows you draw on the chalkboard.

Coach: That's only one part of the game. You have no problem understanding those tactics. It's the other part I'm worried about.

Corey: What other part?

Coach: You don't play with your brain, Corey. You play with your emotions.

Corey: But all the best players get emotional about the game!

Coach: The best players, Corey, learn other kinds of tactics— ways to control their anger on the field—and off.

Corey: (dejected) The season is over. What does it matter now?

Coach: There's always next year, and after that, you could play in high school. You're that good. But they're not going to start someone they can't count on.

Corey: So . . . You don't think they'd play me?

Coach: That'll be up to you.

Narrator 2: Becca is waiting for Corey when he walks out of the locker room. She hands him a banana.

Becca: I brought you this. You need your potassium.

Narrator 3: Becca's loyalty nearly makes him cry. He swallows hard.

Corey: I'm sorry if I embarrassed you at the game today.

Becca: It's okay. It's just a game.

Narrator 1: Corey realizes then that it isn't just a game. He hasn't embarrassed just his teammates or Becca. Most of all, he has embarrassed himself.

Scene 7

Narrator 2: On Monday morning, Corey knocks on the Coach's door.

Corey: Hey, Coach. You think you could teach me some of that anger-control stuff?

Coach: You sure you're ready to talk—and to listen?

Corey: Yeah, I think I'd better learn how to keep my cool so I can play in high school.

Coach: Good! Let's get started.

The End

Think It Over

1. Find examples in Scenes 1, 2, and 3 where Corey has difficulty controlling his anger. What causes him to become angry at these times?

2. Describe the relationship between Corey and his sister Becca. How does Corey both encourage—and discourage—his sister when it comes to playing soccer?

3. In Scene 4, what does Becca mean when she says Corey embarrasses her? How does he do this and why would his behavior hurt Becca?

4. What is the difference between jealousy and anger? Is Corey jealous of or angry at Paul Iorio? Give a reason to support your answer.

5. Coach tells Corey that he can learn "anger-control tactics," or ways to control his emotions. But Coach asks Corey first if he is ready to listen. What does listening have to do with controlling your anger?

6. Do you believe Corey will change? Why or why not?

7. The title of this book is *Flashpoints!* What is Corey's flashpoint?

Home Rules

Monica knows how to get her way—by lashing out at those who oppose her, especially her older sister. Now the way she is behaving has begun affecting her parents as well. With the help of a friend, the family works together to help Monica be accountable for her behavior.

Characters:

Narrators 1, 2, 3

Monica Esposito, a 12-year-old girl

Jessica Esposito, Monica's older sister

Mrs. Esposito, Monica's mother

Mr. Esposito, Monica's father

Sara, Monica's friend

Toby, Jessica's co-worker at Burger Bungalow

Scene 1

Narrator 1: Grandma Esposito's family is holding a surprise party for her birthday. But the family's plans for a relaxing weekend in the country are disrupted by their 12-year-old daughter, Monica.

Monica: I'm not going.

Mrs. Esposito: The whole family is going to be there. Grandma wants to see you!

Monica: She doesn't even know we're having a party for her, so how can she want to see me? Besides, Jessica is staying home. Why can't I?

Jessica: Because you're 12. Because I have a job, and I have to work this weekend. I'm not staying home to babysit you.

Narrator 2: "Baby." This word is one of the flashpoints in the sisters' relationship. Monica's temper explodes.

Monica: I don't need you to watch me. You need me to watch you! *(to her mother)* You have no idea what goes on here while you're at work.

Mrs. Esposito: *(to Jessica)* What goes on?

Jessica: Oh, please! You're going to listen to her?

Monica: Ask her about JA-son!

Mrs. Esposito: Does Jason come over here when I'm at work? You know the home rules: No boys when Dad and I aren't home.

Narrator 3: Once again, Monica has succeeded in shifting the focus of the argument away from herself and onto her sister.

Narrator 1: Later that night, their mother and father talk privately.

Mr. Esposito: So you agreed to let her stay home?

Mrs. Esposito: Well, she *is* getting older. She thinks we trust Jessica and not her.

Mr. Esposito: Monica's right. We don't trust her.

Mrs. Esposito: But, David, it's time. Monica has to learn responsibility, too.

19

Mr. Esposito: We didn't leave Jessica alone at 12.

Mrs. Esposito: Monica won't be alone. Jessica will be here.

Mr. Esposito: That's what worries me. When those two are alone together, there are fireworks!

Mrs. Esposito: Monica is not a kid anymore, but she's not a teenager, either. It's not easy for her. Besides, I'm really tired of having these battles with her!

Mr. Esposito: Either you are a very understanding mother or our youngest daughter has you wrapped around her finger!

Scene 2

Narrator 2: On Saturday morning, the sisters wave goodbye to their parents.

Mr. Esposito: Remember. Monica, no fighting! No friends! Jessica, no boys!

Narrator 3: An hour later, Jessica dresses in her uniform for her afternoon shift at Burger Bungalow.

Narrator 1: When she comes downstairs, she sees her sister and her sister's friend Sara having snacks.

Jessica: You can't stay, Sara. I have to go to work now.

Monica: Why does Sara have to leave?

Jessica: Because nobody will be here. It's the home rules. No friends.

Monica: No boy friends! And since I don't have any, mom and dad were talking about you!

Jessica: Monica, you know what they said. Don't twist their words.

Sara: Why don't you come to my house? We'll go swimming.

Jessica: No, Monica wanted to stay home. So she's going to stay home. Alone.

Narrator 2: Monica picks up her soda and throws it at her sister. The soda splashes over Jessica's uniform.

Monica: You're always bossing me around!

Narrator 3: Jessica has no time to change or she'll be late. She opens the door to leave.

Jessica: You'd better be here when I get back!

Scene 3

Jessica: *(at work, to Toby)* She's so immature. I hate her.

Toby: No, you don't. You just hate the way she makes you feel. If you stay in control of your feelings and don't get angry, she doesn't win. It's that simple.

Jessica: With Monica, *nothing* is simple. She argues about doing the dishes, about whose turn it is to shower first in the morning before school. Everything!

Toby: You ever hear that saying, don't sweat the small stuff? Well, that's what this is—small stuff. Don't let it bother you. Just take a deep breath and say, "Small stuff."

Jessica: Right. You try living with her 24/7!

Scene 4

Narrator 1: At five o'clock that evening . . .

Jessica: Monica? I'm home. Are you hungry? I brought burgers and salads.

Narrator 2: The house is quiet.

Jessica: *(calling louder)* Monica? *(to herself)* Okay, calm down. So she didn't listen to you and went to Sara's. *(takes a deep breath)* Small stuff. Small stuff.

Narrator 3: Jessica turns on the television but finds she can't concentrate. After 20 minutes, she dials Sara's number. No one answers.

Narrator 1: Fifteen minutes later, she calls again. Still, no answer.

Narrator 2: At six o'clock the telephone rings.

Jessica:	Hello.
Mrs. Esposito:	How are things going? No fights I hope.
Jessica:	Ah, not right now. It's . . . quiet.
Narrator 3:	It's not really a lie. Without Monica in the house, things are quiet.
Jessica:	Having a good time? Was grandma surprised?
Mrs. Esposito:	You should have seen her face. *(pause)* Are you okay?
Jessica:	I'm fine. Just a little tired from work.
Narrator 1:	After she hangs up the telephone, Jessica begins to worry. Maybe something has happened. She goes out to look for her sister.

Scene 5

Narrator 2:	At eight o'clock, Jessica returns home, alone. The house is still empty. She is truly frightened now. Toby said don't sweat the small stuff. But this isn't small stuff.
Narrator 3:	She picks up the telephone and calls Toby, who is still on duty.
Jessica:	Monica's gone!
Toby:	Gone where?
Jessica:	That's just it. I don't know. Do you think she ran away?
Toby:	Monica might want to make you mad or get even with you, but I don't think she'd run away. She's probably just staying away because she knows it'll get you angry.
Jessica:	Maybe she's hurt! Should I call the police?
Toby:	I'm sure she's okay, but if you're concerned, you should call your parents.
Narrator 1:	Jessica does just that. Her mother and father are a three-hour drive away. They can hear the panic in Jessica's voice.

Jessica: It's almost nine o'clock and she's not home. I don't know where she is. What do I do?

Mr. Esposito: Stay there. Your mother and I are on our way.

Scene 6

Narrator 2: At 9:30, the front door opens. Monica waves to Sara's parents, who have driven her home.

Jessica: Where were you?

Monica: Sara's parents took us to a movie.

Narrator 3: Jessica's fear subsides. Her sister is safe. But another emotion now surges through her: anger.

Narrator 1: Jessica really feels like yelling at Monica, but she is also determined not to lose control. She stares hard at Monica.

Jessica: *(in a very tense voice)* You couldn't call me at work to tell me?

Monica: You would have said no.

Jessica: You couldn't leave a note?

Monica: I have friends, too! Why does no one ever think about what I might want? I have my own life, you know.

Narrator 2: She runs to her room and slams the door.

Narrator 3: Jessica gets on the phone and tries calling her parents, but she keeps getting a busy signal.

Narrator 1: After midnight, the girls' parents arrive home. Jessica, who had fallen asleep on the couch, is now in the kitchen. She has been crying. At first, her parents suspect the worst—something terrible has happened to Monica.

Jessica: She's in her room. She's okay. She went to the movies with Sara's parents. I think she knew I'd call you and then you'd be angry with me.

Mr. Esposito: We're not angry with you. And you were right to call.

Jessica: She does it every time. She starts a fight to get her own way. Mom, I was really scared!

Mrs. Esposito: It's okay now. We're home. Everyone's safe. That's the important thing.

Mr. Esposito: I'm going to talk to Monica right now.

Mrs. Esposito: No. You're too angry. And we're both too tired from the drive. We need to talk, but in the morning, when we've had time to think.

Scene 7

Narrator 2: In the morning, the family sits around the kitchen table.

Mr. Esposito: I can't put up with this fighting and defiance any longer.

Monica: I'm sorry. I didn't mean to ruin the party for you guys.

Mrs. Esposito: This isn't about your father and me, or even your grandmother's party. This is about your behavior. You could have called your sister, but you didn't. Why, Monica?

Monica: I don't know.

Mrs. Esposito: I think you do.

Monica: I was angry, okay? I wanted her to worry, to be sorry for making me stay home alone.

Mr. Esposito: Actions have consequences. That means you have to be accountable for your actions. Monica, don't you realize we were trusting you?

Monica: So what are you going to do? Ground me?

Narrator 3: Her father slides a piece of paper to the center of the table. On the top is written "Home Rules Contract."

Monica: More rules?

Mr. Esposito: Same rules, but this list has consequences. And you are both going to sign it.

Narrator 1: Jessica and Monica are looking away, uninterested.

Monica: What about this...? Why not let Jessica and me make up the consequences?

Narrator 2: Despite herself, Jessica laughs.

Mrs. Esposito: Monica has a point. If the girls help make up the rules and the consequences, then they might be more likely to stick by them.

Monica: So we both get a say in what the rule should be? I mean, not just Jessica, but me, too?

Mrs. Esposito: Yes.

Narrator 3: Mr. Esposito reaches for a fresh, clean sheet of paper.

Mr. Esposito: Okay, rule number one. Curfew. What are the consequences for breaking curfew?

Monica: Being grounded for a day.

Mr. Esposito: No way, Monica. Two weeks.

Monica: One week?

Mrs. Esposito: I could live with that. Write it down.

Narrator 1: The Espositos work on the list together. It is the first step toward a family communicating better and living together—without so much drama.

The End

Think It Over

1. In Scene 1, Mr. Esposito says either his wife is a very understanding mother or their daughter has her wrapped around her finger. In your opinion, which is it? Provide a reason for your response.

2. Describe the relationship between Monica and Jessica. Do the sisters truly dislike one another? How do you know?

3. Jessica experiences both fear for and anger at her sister. What is the difference between fear and anger?

4. Monica's father says that people must be accountable for their actions. What were the consequences of Monica not telling her sister where she was? What should be her punishment for this action?

5. Does Monica regret her actions? Explain why you do or do not think so.

6. The play ends with the parents and the children writing a list of home rules together. Do you think this strategy will work? Will Monica pay more attention to the rules if she has a say in them—and the punishments for breaking them? Explain why you do or do not think so.

Your Turn

1. With a partner or partners, create a four-page booklet titled *Anger-Control Tactics*. In this booklet list six to ten strategies for controlling angry outbursts. First, go to your library to find books or articles about controlling anger. You might also hunt for anger-management tips online at various Web sites. Here are two sites for you to look at:

kidshealth.org/kid/feeling/emotion/anger.html
www.angermanagementtips.com/teens.htm

Finally, you might interview some adults and students in your school about how they control their anger. When you have completed your research, write and design your booklet.

2. Write a paper about yourself and your flashpoints. What is it—a word or an action—that is sure to trigger your temper? Describe what happens and why and how you can attempt to control your anger.

Glossary

accountable Responsible

aggressive Bold, ready to attack or confront

consequence A result, a relationship between cause and effect

flashpoint A critical stage in some process or event, a moment or place where violence is likely to break out suddenly

immature Showing behavior or emotions that would be more typical of someone younger

lateral Side

ligament A band of tissue that connects bones and supports a muscle

striker In soccer, the position of forward or attacker; a player whose job is to move the ball toward the goal and score

subside To lessen, recede, become less intense

tactics Plans, strategies

About the Author

Catherine Gourley is the author of the award-winning nonfiction series *Women's Images and Issues of the 20th Century: How Popular Culture Portrayed Women in the 20th Century*. She is the national director of Letters About Literature, a reading promotion program of the Center for the Book in the Library of Congress.